CONTENTS

25 READINGS FOR ADVENT

The COMING of the KING

COMPILED & EDITED BY MARY DAVIS

J C RYLE

10 Publishing
a division of 10ofthose.com

Devotional material (lightly edited) is taken from Graham Hind (ed.), *J C Ryle: Expository Thoughts* (Matthew and Luke), Evangelical Press. Prayers © Mary Davis.

British Library Cataloguing in Publication Data
A record for this book is available from the British Library

ISBN: 978-1-914966-79-8

Designed and typeset by Pete Barnsley (CreativeHoot.com)

Cover background image: Rinck Content Studio on unsplash

Printed in Denmark

10Publishing, a division of 10ofthose.com
Unit C, Tomlinson Road, Leyland, PR25 2DY, England

Email: info@10ofthose.com
Website: www.10ofthose.com

1 3 5 7 10 8 6 4 2

INTRODUCTION

For most of us, Advent is synonymous with Christmas. After all, don't our Advent calendars and candles help us to count down to December 25th? Isn't Advent a time to think about the birth of the baby in the manger, the angels and the shepherds? It certainly is. The word "advent" means a "coming" or "arrival"—in particular, the coming of the special baby who was laid in a manger in Bethlehem 2,000 years ago.

But J C Ryle, who was Bishop of Liverpool in the late 1800s, would often remind people of the "Second Advent" when Jesus will come again. On that day, Jesus will return to our world, not as a baby but as the unmistakable King of kings and Lord of lords.

The Church of England's official Prayer Book that Ryle used was the 1662 *Book of Common Prayer*. In it, the Collect (or prayer) for the First Sunday in Advent speaks both of Jesus' first advent—when human eyes first saw the Son of God—and his second, when he will come again in glory. In these 25 readings, we will also consider the two advents of Christ, in the hope it will deepen our understanding of both. In Ryle's words:

> *[Jesus Christ] came the first time as a man of sorrows and acquainted with grief, He was born in the manger of Bethlehem, in lowliness and humiliation ... He will come the second time as the King of all the earth, with all royal majesty.*

1

These readings are all from Ryle's *Expository Thoughts*, from the Gospels of Matthew and Luke. Our first two reflections contrast Jesus' first coming with his second. Then 9 reflections which consider the second advent, taken from Matthew's Gospel; and 14 readings on the first advent from Luke's Gospel, taking us right up to Christmas Day. Ryle's theology and distinctive style have been retained and his original language lightly updated for today's readers. I have also added a prayer to each reading to aid our devotions.

The first time I read Ryle's reflections on the Gospels many years ago, I was thrilled by his warm, single-minded, contagious devotion to Jesus. Even though his material is well over 100 years old, his words remain as relevant, fresh and heart-warming as ever. I think it is because Ryle himself is so focused on our Lord Jesus, who doesn't change, and because he speaks directly to the human heart which is essentially unchanged since the time of our forebears in the garden of Eden.

I hope your heart will be warmed, as mine is, by Ryle's effusive meditations on our Lord Jesus Christ. But be warned—he is uncompromising as he explains the implications of Jesus' second coming as King. He doesn't steer clear of passages about our Lord's return that we may find hard to hear.

Finally, in these words, we see Ryle's heartbeat:

My chief aim ... in all my writings is to exalt the Lord Jesus Christ and make him beautiful and glorious in the eyes of men, and to promote the increase of repentance, faith, and holiness on earth.

AN ADVENT PRAYER

ALMIGHTY God,
give us grace
that we may cast away the works of darkness,
and put upon us the armour of light,
now in the time of this mortal life,
in which thy Son Jesus Christ
came to visit us in great humility;
that in the last day,
when he shall come again in his glorious Majesty,
to judge both the quick and the dead,
we may rise to the life immortal;
through him who liveth and reigneth
with thee and the Holy Ghost,
now and ever.
Amen.

The Collect for the first Sunday in Advent,
Book of Common Prayer, 1662

THE TWO ADVENTS OF CHRIST

He came the first time in weakness,
a tender infant born of a poor woman
in the manger at Bethlehem,
unnoticed, unhonoured and scarcely known.

He shall come the second time in royal dignity,
with the armies of heaven around Him,
to be known, recognised
and feared by all the people of the earth.

—J C Ryle, *Expository Thoughts (Mark's Gospel)*

KING OF KINGS

READ MATTHEW 24:29–35

"The sun will be darkened, and the moon will not give its light; the stars will fall from heaven, and the powers of the heavens will be shaken. Then the sign of the Son of Man will appear in heaven, and then all the tribes of the earth will mourn, and they will see the Son of Man coming on the clouds of heaven with power and great glory." (24:29–30)

In this part of our Lord's prophecy He describes His own second coming. These verses teach us that when the Lord Jesus returns to this world, He will come with particular glory and majesty. He will come "in the clouds of heaven with power and great glory." Before His presence the very sun, moon and stars will be darkened, and "the powers of the heavens will be shaken."

The second personal coming of Christ will be as different as possible from the first. He came the first time as a man of sorrows and acquainted with grief, He was born in the manger of Bethlehem, in lowliness and humiliation. He took on him the form of a servant, and was despised and rejected by mankind. He was betrayed into the hands of wicked people, condemned by an unjust judgment, mocked, scourged, crowned with thorns and, at last, crucified between two thieves.

He will come the second time as the King of all the earth, with all royal majesty. The princes and great men of this world will themselves stand before His throne to receive an eternal sentence. Before Him every mouth will be stopped, every knee bow and every tongue will confess that Jesus Christ is Lord.

May we all remember this. Whatever ungodly men and women may do now, there will be no scoffing, no jesting at Christ, no infidelity at the last day. The servants of Jesus may well wait patiently. Their master will one day be acknowledged King of kings by all the world.

PRAYER

Lord of lords, King of kings, you came into our world in lowliness and humiliation. You were despised, rejected, betrayed, condemned and crucified. But, one day you will return as King of all the earth. I worship you today and I acknowledge you as King of my life. As I wait for that day, show me how I am rejecting you as King of my life. I turn my heart back to you now. Amen.

DECEMBER 2

WHEN HE COMES IN HIS GLORY

READ MATTHEW 25:31–46

"When the Son of Man comes in His glory, and all the holy angels with Him, then He will sit on the throne of His glory." (25:31)

In these verses our Lord Jesus Christ describes the Judgment Day and some of its leading circumstances. There are few passages in the whole Bible more solemn and heart-searching than this. May we read it with the deep and serious attention which it deserves.

Let us mark who will be the Judge in the last day—we read that it will be the Son of Man, Jesus Christ Himself.

That same Jesus who was born in the manger of Bethlehem and took upon Him the form of a servant, who was despised and rejected of men and often had no place to lay His head, who was condemned by the princes of this world, beaten, scourged and nailed to the cross: that same Jesus shall Himself judge the world, when He comes in His glory. To Him the Father has committed all judgment (John 5:22). To Him at last every knee shall bow, and every tongue confess that He is Lord (Philippians 2:10–11).

Let believers think of this and take comfort. He that sits upon the throne in that great and dreadful day will be their Saviour, their Shepherd, their High Priest, their elder Brother, their Friend. When they see Him, they will have no cause to be alarmed.

Let unconverted people think of this and be afraid. Their judge will be that same Christ whose gospel they now despise and whose gracious invitations they refuse to hear. How great will be their confusion at last, if they go on in unbelief and die in their sins! To be condemned in the day of judgment by anyone would be awful, but to be condemned by Him who would have saved them will be awful indeed. Well may the Psalmist say, "Kiss the Son, lest He be angry" (Psalm 2:12).

PRAYER

Lord Jesus Christ, one day, every knee will bow and every tongue confess that you are Lord. One day I will face you as my Judge— but you are also my Saviour, my Shepherd, my High Priest, my elder Brother and my Friend. I praise you for your indescribable mercy and grace.

I pray for *(name a friend or family member)* who has not yet bowed the knee to you. I pray that you would open the eyes of their heart to see you for who you truly are. Amen.

THE
SECOND
ADVENT

Above all, let us long for our Lord's return.
Oh! for a heart to pray daily, "Come, Lord Jesus!"

—J C Ryle, *Expository Thoughts (Matthew's Gospel)*

A MULTITUDE THAT NO ONE CAN COUNT

READ MATTHEW 24:29–35

"The sun will be darkened, and the moon will not give its light; the stars will fall from heaven, and the powers of the heavens will be shaken. Then the sign of the Son of Man will appear in heaven, and then all the tribes of the earth will mourn, and they will see the Son of Man coming on the clouds of heaven with power and great glory. And He will send His angels with a great sound of a trumpet, and they will gather together His elect from the four winds, from one end of heaven to the other." (24:29–31)

These verses teach us that when Christ returns to this world, He will first take care of His believing people: "He will send His angels … and they will gather together His elect."

In the day of judgment, true Christians will be perfectly safe. Not a hair of their heads shall fall to the ground, not one bone of Christ's mystical body shall be broken. There was an ark for Noah in the day of the flood, the city of Zoar for Lot when Sodom was destroyed. There will be a hiding-place for all believers in Jesus when the wrath of God at last bursts on this wicked world. Those mighty angels who rejoiced in heaven when each sinner repented will gladly catch up the people of Christ to meet their Lord in the air. That day, no doubt, will be an awful day, but believers may look forward to it without fear.

In the day of judgment true Christians will at length be gathered together, the saints of every age and every language will be assembled out of every land. All will be there, from righteous Abel down to the last soul that is converted to God, from the oldest patriarch down to the little infant that just breathed and died. Let us think what a happy gathering that will be, when all the family of God are finally together. If it has been pleasant to meet one or two saints occasionally on earth, how much more pleasant will it be to meet a multitude that no one can count! Surely we may be content to carry the cross and put up with partings for a few years. We travel on towards a day when we will meet to part no more.

PRAYER

Lord, I confess that talk of judgment is hard to understand and rather terrifying. Thank you for the promise that you will send your angels to gather the elect. Thank you that followers of Jesus will be safe on that dreadful day. Help me to live wholeheartedly for you in gratitude for this wonderful rescue. Lord, I pray that you would pour out your love into the hearts of my friends and family who do not know you. May they be part of the multitude that no one can count, gathering around your throne. Amen.

MY WORDS WILL NEVER PASS AWAY

READ MATTHEW 24:29–35

"Heaven and earth will pass away, but My words will by no means pass away." (24:35)

These verses also teach us that our Lord's predictions will certainly be fulfilled. He says, "Heaven and earth will pass away, but my words will by no means pass away."

Our Lord knew well the natural unbelief of human nature. He knew that scoffers would arise in the last days, saying, "Where is the promise of His coming?" (2 Peter 3:3–4). He knew that when He came, faith would be rare on the earth. He foresaw how many would contemptuously reject the solemn predictions He had just been delivering as improbable, unlikely and absurd.

He warns us all against such sceptical thoughts with a caution of particular seriousness. He tells us that whatever people may say or think, His words will be fulfilled in their season and shall not pass away unaccomplished.

May we all lay to heart His warning. We live in an unbelieving age; few believed the report of our Lord's first coming and few believe the report of His second (Isaiah 53:1). Let us beware of this infection and believe so that our souls may be saved. We are not reading cunningly devised fables but deep and momentous truths. May God give us a heart to believe them.

PRAYER

Gracious Lord, we live in an unbelieving age. Few people consider the importance of your life and death 2,000 years ago. Even fewer believe that you will come again. Fill my heart with confidence in the truth and power of your word once again this Christmas. As I think about your birth and your return, remind me of the life-changing truths of the gospel and give me increasing confidence in the power of the gospel to save and restore. Amen.

A DREADFUL DAY

READ MATTHEW 24:36–51

"But of that day and hour no one knows, not even the angels of heaven, but My Father only. But as the days of Noah were, so also will the coming of the Son of Man be. For as in the days before the flood, they were eating and drinking, marrying and giving in marriage … Then two men will be in the field: one will be taken and the other left." (24:36–38, 40)

The first thing that demands our attention in these verses is the awful account that they give of the state of the world when the Lord Jesus comes again.

The world will not be converted when Christ returns. It will be found in the same condition that it was in the day of the flood. When the flood came, men were found "eating and drinking, marrying and giving in marriage," absorbed in their worldly pursuits and utterly deaf to Noah's repeated warnings. They saw no likelihood of a flood and they would not believe there was any danger, but at last the flood came suddenly and took them all away. All that were not with Noah in the ark were drowned. They were all swept away to their last account, unpardoned, unconverted and unprepared to meet God. And our Lord says, "so also will the coming of the Son of Man be."

The second thing that demands our attention is the awful separation that will take place when the Lord Jesus comes again. We read twice over that "one will be taken and the other left."

The godly and the ungodly at present are all mixed together. In the congregation and in the place of worship, in the city and in the field, the children of God and the children of the world are all side by side. But it will not be so always. In the day of our Lord's return, there will be a complete division. In a moment, in the twinkling of an eye, at the last trumpet, one shall be separated from the other for evermore. Wives shall be separated from husbands, parents from children, brothers from sisters, preachers from hearers. There will be no time for parting words or a change of mind when the Lord appears. All will be taken as they are, and reap according as they have sown. Believers will be caught up to glory, honour and eternal life, unbelievers will be left behind to shame and everlasting contempt. Blessed and happy are they who are of one heart in following Christ! Their union will never be broken, it will last for evermore. Who can describe the happiness of those who are taken when the Lord returns? Who can imagine the misery of those who are left behind? May we think on these things and consider our ways.

PRAYER

Almighty and Ever-living God, Holy and Majestic Lord, Maker of the heavens and the earth, you are the King of kings and Lord of lords. Have mercy on those who are far from you. Draw them back from death to life and may I be generous in sharing the good news of forgiveness with those who don't know you. Help me to order my life and priorities in the light of these truths. May I be faithful in following you, Lord of all the earth. Amen.

DECEMBER 6

WATCH AND PRAY

READ MATTHEW 24:36–51

"Watch therefore, for you do not know what hour your Lord is coming ... Therefore you also be ready, for the Son of Man is coming at an hour you do not expect." (24:42, 44)

Something that demands our attention in these verses is the practical duty of watchfulness in the prospect of Christ's second coming. "Watch therefore," says our Lord, "for you do not know what hour your Lord is coming," and "be ready, for the Son of Man is coming at an hour you do not expect."

This is a point which our blessed Master frequently presses upon our notice. We hardly ever find Him dwelling on His second advent without adding a warning to watch. He knows the sleepiness of our nature; He knows how soon we forget the most important subjects in our faith. He knows how unceasingly Satan labours to obscure the glorious doctrine of His coming again. He arms us with heart-searching exhortations to keep awake, if we desire not to be ruined for evermore. May we all have an ear to hear them.

True Christians ought to live like watchmen. The day of the Lord comes like a thief in the night, so Christians should strive to be always on their guard. They should behave like the guard of an army in an enemy's land—they should resolve by God's grace not to sleep at their post. That text of Paul deserves much thought: "let us not sleep, as others do, but let us watch and be sober" (1 Thessalonians 5:6).

True Christians ought to live like good servants whose master is not at home. They should strive to be always ready for their master's return. They should never give way to the feeling, "my Lord delays His coming." They should seek to keep their hearts in such a state that whenever Christ appears, they may at once give Him a warm and loving reception. There is a vast depth in that saying, "Blessed is that servant whom his master, when he comes, will find so doing." We may well doubt whether we are true believers in Jesus if we are not ready at any time to have our faith changed into sight.

Let us close with serious feelings. The things we have just been reading call loudly for great searchings of heart. Let us seek to make sure that we are in Christ and have an ark of safety when the day of wrath breaks on the world.

PRAYER

Righteous Lord, you tell me to watch and be ready. Help me to live as an attentive sentry, on my guard, not asleep at my post. I confess that I am so easily distracted by the worries and pleasures of this life. In the quietness of this moment, reveal to me where I have taken my eyes off you. Help me to live as a faithful servant whose master is not at home, ready to give him a warm and loving reception when he returns. May I have an ark of safety when the day of wrath breaks on the world. May those I love and pray for wake up to these truths. Amen.

A GUEST AT THE WEDDING FEAST

READ MATTHEW 25:1–13

"The kingdom of heaven shall be likened to ten virgins who took their lamps and went out to meet the bridegroom. Now five of them were wise, and five were foolish ... the wise took oil in their vessels with their lamps ... the bridegroom came, and those who were ready went in with him to the wedding; and the door was shut." (25:1–2, 4, 10)

We see in this parable that when Christ returns, true Christians will receive a rich reward for all they have suffered for their Master's sake. We are told that when the bridegroom came, "those who were ready went in with him to the wedding; and the door was shut."

Only true Christians will be found ready at the second advent. Washed in the blood of atonement, clothed in Christ's righteousness, renewed by the Spirit, they will meet their Lord with boldness and sit down at the marriage supper of the Lamb, to go out no more. Surely this is a blessed prospect.

They will be with their Lord, with Him who loved them and gave Himself for them, with Him who bore with them and carried them through their earthly pilgrimage, with Him whom they loved truly and followed faithfully on earth, though with much weakness and many a tear. Surely this also is a blessed prospect.

The door will be shut at last: shut on all pain and sorrow, shut on an ill-natured and wicked world, shut on a tempting devil, shut on all doubts and fears, shut, never to be opened again. Surely, we may again say, this is a blessed prospect.

Let us remember these things. They will bear meditation; they are all true. The believer may have much tribulation, but great consolations lie ahead. Heaviness may endure for a night, but joy comes in the morning. The day of Christ's return will surely make amends for all.

Let us leave this parable with a settled determination never to be content with anything short of indwelling grace in our hearts. The lamp and the name of Christian, the profession and the observances of Christianity are all well in their way, but they are not the one thing needed. Let us never rest till we know that we have the oil of the Spirit in our hearts.

PRAYER

Jesus our Bridegroom, you invite us to your wedding feast. What joy will be ours! What a blessed prospect! I am so grateful today that I have this certain hope. I pray that you would encourage those who follow you who are in the midst of difficulties right now. Remind them of the joy that awaits us on that day. Fill us with the oil of your Spirit in our hearts that we may love you and serve you until you come again. Amen.

BE WATCHFUL!

READ MATTHEW 25:1–13

"Then the kingdom of heaven shall be likened to ten virgins who took their lamps and went out to meet the bridegroom ... while the bridegroom was delayed, they all slumbered and slept. And at midnight a cry was heard: 'Behold, the bridegroom is coming; go out to meet him!' ... Watch therefore, for you know neither the day nor the hour in which the Son of Man is coming." (25:1, 5–6, 13)

The parable of the ten virgins contains lessons especially serious and awakening. Let us see what they are. We see that Christ's second coming, whenever it may be, will take people by surprise.

This is a truth which is set before us in the parable in a very striking manner. At midnight, when the virgins were slumbering and sleeping, there was a cry, "Behold, the bridegroom is coming; go out to meet him!" It will be just the same when Jesus returns to the world. He will find the vast majority of mankind utterly unbelieving and unprepared. He will find the bulk of His believing people in a sleepy and lazy state of soul. Business will be going on in town and country, just as it does now. Politics, trades, farming, buying, selling, pleasure-seeking will be taking up people's attention just as they do now. Rich men will still be doing very well and poor men murmuring and complaining. Churches will still be full of divisions and wrangling about small things and theological controversies will be still raging. Ministers will still be calling men and women to repent and congregations still putting off the day of decision.

In the midst of all this the Lord Jesus Himself will suddenly appear. In an hour when no one thinks, the startled world will be summoned to break off all its employments and to stand before its lawful King. There is something unspeakably awful in the idea, but thus it is written and thus it shall be. Well might a minister say, "we are none of us more than half-awake."

PRAYER

Father in heaven, I know neither the day nor the hour when your Son will come. Forgive me for my sleepy, lazy soul. Wake me up so that I live each day with your kingdom priorities, sharing the hope and love that you offer with everyone I meet. May the reality of Jesus' return shape my life. It could be today! Amen.

GOD'S STEWARDS

READ MATTHEW 25:14–30

"For the kingdom of heaven is like a man traveling to a far country, who called his own servants and delivered his goods to them. And to one he gave five talents, to another two, and to another one, to each according to his own ability; and immediately he went on a journey." (25:14–15)

The parable of the talents is very close to that of the ten virgins. Both direct our minds to the same important event, the second advent of Jesus Christ. Both bring before us the same persons, the members of the professing church of Christ. Vigilance is the key note of the first parable, diligence that of the second. The story of the virgins calls on the church to watch, the story of the talents calls on the church to work.

We learn from this parable that all professing Christians have received something from God. We are all God's servants. We all have "talents" entrusted to our charge. In the sense in which our Lord used the word in this parable, it applies to all baptised persons without distinction. We all have talents in God's sight, we are all talented people. Anything with which we may glorify God is a talent: our gifts, our influence, our money, our knowledge, our health, our strength, our time, our senses, our reason, our intellect, our memory, our affections, our privileges as members of Christ's church, our advantages as possessors of the Bible—all are talents.

Where did these things come from? What hand bestowed them? There is only one answer to these questions. All that we have is a loan from God. We are God's stewards. We are God's debtors. Let this thought sink deeply into our hearts.

PRAYER

Thank you, generous Father, for the gifts and talents you have entrusted me with. I acknowledge that all I have comes from you and I am so grateful. I confess my pride that wants to take credit for my accomplishments, and my laziness that stops me using the gifts you have given me for your purposes. I pray for opportunities today to serve you joyfully with the gifts I have been given. Amen.

GOOD AND FAITHFUL SERVANT

READ MATTHEW 25:14–30

"His lord said to him, 'Well done, good and faithful servant; you were faithful over a few things, I will make you ruler over many things. Enter into the joy of your lord.'" (25:21)

We learn from this parable that true Christians will receive an abundant reward in the great day of reckoning. It tells us that the servants who had used their Lord's money well were commended as "good and faithful" and told to enter into the joy of their Lord.

These words are full of comfort to all believers and may well fill us with wonder and surprise. The best of Christians is a poor frail creature and needs the blood of atonement every day that he or she lives. But the least and lowest of believers will find that they are counted among Christ's servants and that their labour has not been wasted in the Lord's service. They will discover to their amazement that their Master's eye saw more beauty in their efforts to please Him than they ever saw themselves. They will find that every hour spent in Christ's service and every word spoken on Christ's behalf has been written in a book of remembrance.

Let believers remember these things and take courage. The cross may be heavy now, but the glorious reward will make amends for all. Here some drops of joy may enter into us, but there we shall enter into joy.

Let us leave this parable with a serious determination, by God's grace, never to be content with a profession of Christianity without practice. Let us not only talk about faith, but act. Let us not only feel the importance of believing, but do something too. We are not told that the unprofitable servant was a murderer, or a thief, or even a waster of his Lord's money. But he did nothing and this was his ruin. Let us beware of a do-nothing Christianity. Such Christianity does not come from the Spirit of God. "To do no harm," says Baxter, "is the praise of a stone, not of a man."

PRAYER

Jesus, my Master and Lord, save me from do-nothing Christianity. Fill me with your Spirit to empower me to serve you today. Everything I have comes from you. Help me to use what you have given me until that day when you return. Lord, I long to hear those words, "Well done, good and faithful servant," and to enter into your joy. Amen.

YOU ARE THE CHRIST, THE SON OF GOD!

READ MATTHEW 26:57–68

And the high priest answered and said to [Jesus], "I put You under oath by the living God: Tell us if You are the Christ, the Son of God!" Jesus said to him, "It is as you said. Nevertheless, I say to you, hereafter you will see the Son of Man sitting at the right hand of the Power, and coming on the clouds of heaven." (26:63–64)

Let us observe how fully our Lord declared to the Jewish council His own Messiahship and His future coming in glory. The unconverted Jew can never tell us at the present day that his forefathers were left in ignorance that Jesus was the Messiah. The high priest presents a solemn charge under oath. Our Lord's answer is a sufficient reply. He tells the council plainly that He is, "the Christ, the Son of God." He goes on to warn them that though He had not yet appeared in glory, as they expected the Messiah would have done, a day would come when he would do so: "hereafter you will see the Son of Man sitting at the right hand of the Power, and coming on the clouds of heaven." They would yet see the same Jesus of Nazareth, whom they had called before their court, appear in all majesty as King of kings (Revelation 1:7).

It is a striking fact which we should not fail to notice that almost the last word spoken by our Lord to the Jews was a warning prediction about His own second advent. He tells them plainly that they would yet see Him in glory. No doubt he referred to the seventh chapter of Daniel in the language that he used, but He spoke to deaf ears. Unbelief, prejudice, self-righteousness covered them like a thick cloud—never was there such an instance of spiritual blindness. Well may the Church of England litany contain the prayer, "From all blindness, and from hardness of heart, good Lord, deliver us."

PRAYER

Gracious Lord, as you stood before the Jewish council, you declared that you were the Christ, the Son of God. You declared that you would come again in glory. The prospect of your return fills me with awe. I worship you, Lord Jesus. Reveal to me my spiritual blindness and my hardness of heart. Open my eyes and soften my heart that I may see you as you are—in majesty, the King of kings. Amen.

THE
FIRST
ADVENT

We have in these verses, the announcement
of the most marvellous event that ever happened in this world
—the incarnation and birth of our Lord Jesus Christ.

—J C Ryle, *Expository Thoughts (Luke's Gospel)*

DECEMBER 12

LOWLY AND UNASSUMING

READ LUKE 1:26–33

Now in the sixth month the angel Gabriel was sent by God to a city of Galilee named Nazareth, to a virgin betrothed to a man whose name was Joseph, of the house of David. The virgin's name was Mary. (1:26–27)

We should notice in the first place the lowly and unassuming manner in which the Saviour of all humanity came among us. The angel who announced His advent was sent to an obscure town of Galilee, named Nazareth. The woman who was honoured to be our Lord's mother was evidently in a humble position in life. Both in her station and her dwelling-place, there was a complete absence of what the world calls greatness.

We need not hesitate to conclude that there was a wise providence in all this arrangement. The Almighty counsel, which orders all things in heaven and earth, could just as easily have appointed Jerusalem to be the place of Mary's residence as Nazareth, or could as easily have chosen the daughter of some rich scribe to be our Lord's mother, as a poor woman. But it seemed good that it should not be so. The first advent of Messiah was to be an advent of humiliation. That humiliation was to begin even from the time of His conception and birth.

Let us beware of being ashamed of poverty if God lays it upon us. The condition of life which Jesus voluntarily chose ought always to be regarded with holy reverence. The common tendency of the day to bow down before rich men and make an idol of money ought to be carefully resisted and discouraged. The example of our Lord is a sufficient answer to a thousand grovelling ideas about wealth which many assume to be right: "though He was rich, yet for your sakes He became poor" (2 Corinthians 8:9).

Let us admire the amazing condescension of the Son of God. The Heir of all things not only took our nature upon Himself, but took it in the most humbling form possible. It would have been condescension to come on earth as a king and reign. It was a miracle of mercy beyond our comprehension to come on earth as a poor man, to be despised, suffer and die. Let His love constrain us to live not for ourselves, but for Him. Let His example daily bring home to our conscience the words of Scripture: "Do not set your mind on high things, but associate with the humble" (Romans 12:16).

PRAYER

Heir of all things, though you were rich, you became poor for my sake. Though you are the Saviour of mankind, your coming was lowly and unassuming. What condescension! What humility! What love! Help me today to live humbly before you, following your example in preferring the needs of others to my own. Amen.

GLORIOUS AND GREAT

READ LUKE 1:26–33

"He will be great, and will be called the Son of the Highest; and the Lord God will give Him the throne of His father David. And He will reign over the house of Jacob forever, and of His kingdom there will be no end." (1:32–33)

Notice the glorious account of our Lord Jesus Christ which the angel gives to Mary. Every part of the account is full of deep meaning and deserves close attention.

Jesus "will be great," says Gabriel. Of His greatness we know something already. He has brought in a great salvation. He has shown Himself a Prophet greater than Moses. He is a great High Priest. And He will be greater still when He shall be owned as a King.

Jesus "will be called the Son of the Highest," says Gabriel. He was so before He came into the world. Equal to the Father in all things, He was from all eternity the Son of God. But He was to be known and acknowledged as such by the church. The Messiah was to be recognised and worshipped as nothing less than truly God.

"The Lord God will give Him the throne of his father David," says Gabriel, "and He will reign over the house of Jacob forever." The literal fulfilment of this part of the promise is yet to come. Israel is yet to be gathered. The Jews are yet to be restored to their own land and to look to Him, whom they once pierced, as their King and their God. Though the accomplishment of this prediction takes time, we may confidently wait for it. It shall surely come one day and not delay (Habakkuk 2:3).

Finally, says Gabriel, "Of His kingdom there will be no end." Before His glorious kingdom the empires of this world will one day go down and pass away. Like Nineveh, Babylon, Egypt, Tyre and Carthage, they will all come to nothing one day and the saints of the Most High will take the kingdom. Before Jesus every knee will one day bow and every tongue confess that He is Lord. His kingdom alone will prove an everlasting kingdom and His dominion will not pass away (Daniel 7:14, 27).

The true Christian should often dwell on this glorious promise and take comfort in its contents. They have no cause to be ashamed of their Master. Poor and despised as they may often be for the gospel's sake, they may feel assured that they are on the conquering side. The kingdoms of this world will yet become the kingdoms of Christ. In just a little time, He will come and not delay (Hebrews 10:37). For that blessed day let us patiently wait, watch and pray. Now is the time for carrying the cross and for fellowship with Christ's sufferings. The day draws near when Christ will take His great power and reign, and when all who have served Him faithfully will exchange a cross for a crown.

PRAYER

Our great Priest and Prophet, Son of the Highest, everlasting King. Before you were born at Bethlehem, the angel told Mary of your great and glorious rule. One day, the kingdoms of this world will end. Everyone will know that your kingdom is everlasting and that you will rule for ever and ever. I take comfort in that truth today as I live for you in sometimes difficult circumstances. Thank you that it will not always be this way! Help me to wait patiently for that day, to watch and to pray. Amen.

THE WORK OF THE SPIRIT

READ LUKE 1:34–38

And the angel answered and said to her, "The Holy Spirit will come upon you, and the power of the Highest will overshadow you; therefore, also, that Holy One who is to be born will be called the Son of God." (1:35)

Let us mark the prominent place assigned to the Holy Spirit in the great mystery of the incarnation. We find it written, "The Holy Spirit will come upon you."

A thoughtful reader of the Bible will probably not fail to remember that the honour here given to the Spirit is in precise harmony with the teaching of Scripture in other places. In every step of the great work of our redemption, we find special mention of the work of the Holy Spirit. Did Jesus die to make atonement for our sins? It is written that "through the eternal Spirit [He] offered Himself without spot to God" (Hebrews 9:14). Did He rise again for our justification? It is written that He was "made alive by the Spirit" (1 Peter 3:18). Does He supply His disciples with comfort between the time of His first and second advent? It is written that the Comforter whom He promised to send is "the Spirit of truth" (John 14:17).

Let us take heed that we give the Holy Spirit the same place in our personal faith which we find Him occupying in God's word. Let us remember that all that believers have, are and enjoy under the gospel, they owe to the inward teaching of the Holy Spirit. The work of each of the three Persons of the Trinity is equally and entirely necessary to the salvation of every saved soul. The election of God the Father, the blood of God the Son and the sanctification of God the Spirit ought never to be separated in our Christianity.

PRAYER

Holy Spirit, Power of the Highest, Blessed member of the Holy Trinity, we honour you. You were active in Creation. You brought about Jesus' glorious resurrection. Day by day, you give new birth to those who trust in Christ.

Heavenly Father, fill me again today with the Spirit of truth that I might know you better and live and work for you. Guide and strengthen and comfort me as I await Jesus' return. Amen.

NOTHING IS TOO HARD FOR HIM

READ LUKE 1:34–38

Then Mary said to the angel, "How can this be, since I do not know a man?" And the angel answered and said to her, "...with God nothing will be impossible." (1:34–35, 37)

Let us mark the mighty principle which the angel Gabriel lays down to silence all objections about the incarnation: "With God nothing will be impossible."

A hearty and eager reception of this great principle is of immense importance to our own inward peace. Questions and doubts will often arise in our minds about many subjects in religion. They are the natural result of our fallen state. Our faith at the best is very feeble. Our knowledge at its highest is clouded with much weakness. And among many antidotes to a doubting, anxious, questioning state of mind, few will be found more useful than that before us now: a thorough conviction of the almighty power of God. With Him who called the world into being and formed it out of nothing, everything is possible. Nothing is too hard for the Lord.

There is no sin too bad to be pardoned—the blood of Christ cleanses from all sin. There is no heart too hard and wicked to be changed—the heart of stone can be made a heart of flesh. There is no work too hard for a believer to do—we may do all things through Christ strengthening us. There is no trial too hard to be borne—the grace of God is sufficient for us. There is no promise too great to be fulfilled—Christ's words never pass away, and what He has promised He is able to perform. There is no difficulty too great for a believer to overcome—when God is for us who will be against us? The mountain will become a plain.

Let principles like these be continually before our minds. The angel's prescription is an invaluable remedy. Faith never rests so calmly and peacefully as when it lays its head on the pillow of God's omnipotence.

PRAYER

Gracious Heavenly Father, with you, nothing is impossible. There is no sin too bad, no heart too wicked, no work or trial too hard. Your grace is sufficient. What you have promised, you are able to perform. If you are for me, who can be against me? I bring before you a situation which seems impossible and I ask you to be at work there. Let me—and those I pray for—lay our heads on the pillow of your omnipotence and trust you in all things today. Amen.

I AM THE LORD'S SERVANT

READ LUKE 1:34–38

Then Mary said, "Behold the maidservant of the Lord! Let it be to me according to your word." (1:38)

Let us mark the meek and ready acceptance of the Virgin Mary in God's revealed will concerning her. She says to the angel, "Behold the maidservant of the Lord! Let it be to me according to your word."

There is far more of admirable grace in this answer than at first sight appears. A moment's reflection will show us that it was no light matter to become the mother of our Lord in this unheard of and mysterious way. It brought with it, no doubt, at a distant period great honour, but it brought with it for the present no small danger to Mary's reputation and no small trial to Mary's faith. All this danger and trial the holy Virgin was willing and ready to risk. She asks no further questions. She raises no further objections. She accepts the honour laid upon her with all its attendant perils and inconveniences. "Behold," she says, "the maidservant of the Lord!"

Let us seek in our daily practical Christianity to exercise the same blessed spirit of faith which we see here in the Virgin Mary. Let us be willing to go anywhere, do anything and be anything, whatever be the present and immediate inconvenience, so long as God's will is clear and the path of duty is plain.

The words of good Bishop Hall on this passage are worth remembering. "All disputations with God, after His will is known, arise from infidelity. There is not a more noble proof of faith than to captivate all the powers of our understanding and will to our Creator, and without all questionings to go blindfold whither He will lead us."

PRAYER

Gracious Lord, thank you for Mary's humble submission to your purposes for her. I am your servant. May your will be done in me and through me, as it was for Mary. Help me to trust and obey you in times of honour and in times of trial, in both joys and in sorrows. Give me obedient faith that loves you and follows you wherever you lead. Amen.

DECEMBER 17

THANKFULNESS AND PRAISE

READ LUKE 1:46–56

"My soul magnifies the Lord, and my spirit has rejoiced in God my Saviour." (1:46–47)

Let us mark the lively thankfulness of the Virgin Mary. It stands out prominently in all the early part of her hymn. Her soul magnifies the Lord. Her spirit rejoices in God. All generations shall call her blessed. Great things have been done for her. We can scarcely enter into the full extent of feelings which a holy Jewish woman would experience on finding herself in Mary's position. But we should try to recollect them as we read her repeated expressions of praise.

We too shall do well to walk in Mary's steps in this matter, and cultivate a thankful spirit. It has ever been a mark of God's most distinguished saints in every age. David in the Old Testament and Paul in the New are remarkable for their thankfulness. We seldom read much of their writings without finding them blessing and praising God. Let us rise from our beds every morning with a deep conviction that we are debtors, and that every day we have more mercies than we deserve. Let us look around us every week as we travel through the world, and see whether we have not much to thank God for. If our hearts are in the right place we shall never find any difficulty in building an Ebenezer (1 Samuel 7:12).[1] Well would it be if our prayers and supplications were more mixed with thanksgiving (Philippians 4:6).

PRAYER

God my Saviour, you have done great things! My soul sings your praises. My spirit rejoices in your love and your grace towards me, a sinner. Your mercies are new every morning. Your kindness to me is so much more than I deserve! May every day of my life be characterised by thankfulness and gratitude to you. Today, throughout the day, help me to notice signs of your grace and turn to you with thanks and praise. Amen.

---

1 Ebenezer means 'Stone of Help', a recognition of God's assistance. Samuel set up a stone to mark the fact that God had helped the Israelites in their battle against the Philistines at Mizpah.

TRUSTING IN GOD'S WORD

READ LUKE 1:46–56

And Mary said: "My soul magnifies the Lord, And my spirit has rejoiced in God my Saviour ... He has helped His servant Israel, in remembrance of His mercy, as He spoke to our fathers, to Abraham and to his seed forever." (1:46–47, 54–55)

Let us mark the full acquaintance with Scripture which this hymn exhibits. It is evident that the memory of the Blessed Virgin was stored with Scripture. She was familiar, whether by hearing or by reading, with the Old Testament. When out of the abundance of her heart her mouth spoke, she gave vent to her feelings in Scriptural language. Moved by the Holy Spirit to break forth into praise, she chooses language which the Holy Spirit had already consecrated and used.

Let us strive, every year we live, to become more deeply acquainted with Scripture. Let us study it, search into it, dig into it, meditate on it, until it dwells in us richly (Colossians 3:16). In particular, let us labour to make ourselves familiar with those parts of the Bible which, like the book of Psalms, describe the experience of the saints of old. We shall find it most helpful to us in all our approaches to God. It will supply us with the best and most suitable language both for the expression of our wants and thanksgivings. Such knowledge of the Bible can doubtless never be attained without regular, daily study, but the time spent on such study is never mis-spent. It will bear fruit after many days.

Let us also mark the firm grasp which the Virgin Mary had of Bible promises. She ends her hymn of praise by declaring that God has "helped His servant Israel in remembrance of His mercy," and that He has done "as He spoke to our fathers, to Abraham and to his seed forever." These words show clearly that she remembered the old promise made to Abraham. Let us learn from her example to lay firm hold on Bible promises. It is of the deepest importance to our peace to do so. Promises are the manna that we should daily eat and the water that we should daily drink, as we travel through the wilderness of this world. We do not see yet all things put under us. We do not see Christ, heaven, the book of life and the mansions prepared for us. We walk by faith and this faith leans on promises, but on those promises we may lean confidently. They will bear all the weight we can lay on them. We shall find one day, like the Virgin Mary, that God keeps His word and that what He has spoken, so He will always in due time perform.

PRAYER

Gracious Lord, may your word dwell in me richly. I confess that I do not give your word the priority it deserves in my life and I do not treasure it as your very word of life to me. May I lay firm hold on all your promises. May they be my food and drink as I travel through the wilderness of this world. As I face troubles, may my instinct be to search your word to know your ways. May I lean confidently on your promises as I walk by faith, knowing that you always keep your word. Amen.

A DEEPLY THANKFUL HEART

READ LUKE 1:67–80

Now [John the Baptist's] father Zacharias was filled with the Holy Spirit, and prophesied, saying: "Blessed is the Lord God of Israel, for He has visited and redeemed His people." (1:67–68)

Let us now read the thanksgiving of Zacharias, the father of John the Baptist, and hear what praise it draws from an aged priest.

We should notice the deep thankfulness of a Jewish believer's heart in the prospect of Messiah's appearing. Praise is the first word that falls from the mouth of Zacharias as soon as his dumbness is removed and his speech restored. He begins with the same expression with which Paul begins several of his letters: "Blessed is the Lord."

At this period of the world we can hardly understand the depth of this good man's feelings. We must imagine ourselves in his position. We must think of ourselves seeing the fulfilment of the oldest promise in the Old Testament, the promise of a Saviour, and beholding the accomplishment of this promise brought near to our own door. We must try to realise what a dim and imperfect view people had of the gospel before Christ actually appeared and the shadows and types passed away.[2] Then perhaps we may have some idea of the feelings of Zacharias when he cried out, "Blessed is the Lord."

It may be feared that Christians have a very low and inadequate understanding of their amazing privileges in living under the full light of the gospel. We have probably a very faint idea of the comparative dimness and twilight of being a Jew before Jesus came. We have a very feeble notion of what the church must have been before the incarnation of Christ. Let us open our eyes to the extent of our obligations. Let us learn from the example of Zacharias to be more thankful.

PRAYER

Blessed Lord God, you have visited and saved your people and our hearts are so thankful for your incredible kindness to us. Long ago, you promised a Saviour—and he has come! You have revealed yourself to us and shared yourself with us. We praise you and thank you. Open my eyes more and more to the wonders of the incarnation. Thank you that in Jesus you have fully revealed yourself to me. Help me not to take it for granted. Amen.

---

2   Types means pattern or hint—like a dress rehearsal for a performance or an architect's plans before a house is built.

GOD FULFILS HIS PROMISES

READ LUKE 1:67–80

"His holy covenant, the oath which He swore to our father Abraham: to grant us that we, being delivered from the hand of our enemies, might serve Him without fear in holiness and righteousness before Him all the days of our life." (1:72–75)

We should notice in this hymn of praise how much stress Zacharias lays on God's fulfilment of His promises. Let us learn to rest on promises and embrace them as Zacharias did. Let us not doubt that every word of God about His people concerning things in the future will as surely be fulfilled as every word about them has been fulfilled concerning things in the past. Their safety is secured by promise. The world, the flesh and the devil will never prevail against any believer. Their acquittal at the last day is secured by promise. They will not come into condemnation, but will be presented spotless before the Father's throne. Their final glory is secured by promise. Their Saviour will come again the second time, as surely as He came the first, to gather His saints together and to give them a crown of righteousness.

Let us be persuaded of these promises. Let us embrace them and not let them go. They will never fail us. God's word is never broken:

He is not human that He should lie. We have a seal on every promise which Zacharias never saw. We have the seal of Christ's blood to assure us that what God has promised, God will perform.

And let us also notice what clear views of Christ's kingdom Zacharias possessed. He declares that the kingdom of Messiah is a kingdom in which His people are to "serve Him without fear, in holiness and righteousness before Him." This kingdom, he proclaimed, was coming near. Prophets had long foretold that it would one day be set up. In the birth of his son John the Baptist and the near approach of Christ, Zacharias saw this kingdom close at hand. Let us give all diligence to belong to this kingdom. Small as it seems now, it will be great and glorious one day. The men and women who have served God in holiness and righteousness will one day see all things put under them. Every enemy will be subdued and they will reign forever in that new heaven and earth, where righteousness dwells.

PRAYER

Father in heaven, your word is never broken. You never lie. Not one of your promises has failed; whatever you say is fulfilled. At the birth of your Son, your kingdom was close at hand. One day, it will be great and glorious and we long for that day when we will reign with you. In the meantime, help me to serve you in holiness and righteousness. Show me how I can serve you today. Amen.

AS THE PROPHETS FORETOLD

READ LUKE 2:1–7

Joseph also went up from Galilee … to the city of David, which is called Bethlehem … to be registered with Mary … who was with child. (2:4–5)

Let us notice the place where Christ was born. It was not at Nazareth of Galilee, where His mother, the Virgin Mary, lived. The prophet Micah had foretold that the event was to take place at Bethlehem (Micah 5:2) and so it came to pass. At Bethlehem Christ was born.

The overruling providence of God appears in this simple fact. He orders all things in heaven and earth. He turns the hearts of kings wherever He will. He overruled the time when Augustus decreed the registration. He directed the enforcement of the decree in such a way that Mary must be at Bethlehem when "the days were completed for her to be delivered." Little did the haughty Roman emperor and his officer Quirinius think that they were only instruments in the hand of the God of Israel, and were only carrying out the eternal purposes of the King of kings. Little did they think that they were helping to lay the foundation of a kingdom before which the empires of this world would all go down one day, and Roman idolatry pass away. The words of Isaiah, upon a similar occasion, should be remembered: "Yet he does not mean so, nor does his heart think so" (Isaiah 10:7).

The heart of a believer should take comfort in the recollection of God's providential government of the world. A true Christian should never be greatly moved or disquieted by the conduct of the rulers of the earth. They should see with the eye of faith a hand overruling all that they do to the praise and glory of God. They should regard every king and potentate—an Augustus, a Quirinius, a Darius, a Cyrus, a Sennacherib—as a creature who with all his power, can do nothing but what God allows and nothing which is not carrying out God's will. And when the rulers of this world set themselves against the Lord, they should take comfort in the truth that though rulers do not know it, there is One higher than them.

PRAYER

Ruler of heaven and earth, you are the Highest King, Lord of All. Human powers may seem mighty—but you are mightier. Human rulers may set themselves against you and your people—but your promises will stand. I pray today for those who are being oppressed or persecuted for their faith by earthly authorities—give them courage to remain faithful to you, knowing that there is One higher than those rulers. Help me and all who love you to trust in your promises to know that you are both powerful and loving. Amen.

NO ROOM IN THE INN

READ LUKE 2:1–7

And she brought forth her firstborn Son, and wrapped Him in swaddling cloths, and laid Him in a manger, because there was no room for them in the inn. (2:7)

Let us notice the manner in which Christ was born. He was not born under the roof of His mother's house, but in a strange place and at an inn. When born, He was not laid in a carefully prepared cradle—He was laid in a manger, because there was no room in the inn.

We see here the grace and condescension of Christ. Had He come to save mankind with royal majesty, surrounded by His Father's angels, it would have been an act of undeserved mercy. Had He chosen to dwell in a palace, with power and great authority, we should have had reason enough to wonder. But to become poor as the very poorest of mankind and lowly as the very lowliest, this is a love that passes knowledge. It is unspeakable and unsearchable. Never let us forget that through this humiliation Jesus has purchased for us a title to glory. Through His life of suffering, as well as His death, He has obtained eternal redemption for us. All through His life He was poor for our sakes, from the hour of His birth to the hour of His death. And through His poverty we are made rich (2 Corinthians 8:9).

Let us beware of despising the poor because of their poverty. Their condition is one which the Son of God has sanctified and honoured by taking it voluntarily on Himself. God does not show partiality. He looks at the hearts of men and women and not at their incomes. Let us never be ashamed of the cross of poverty if God thinks fit to lay it upon us. To be godless and covetous is disgraceful, but it is no disgrace to be poor. A humble dwelling place, coarse food and a hard bed are not pleasing to flesh and blood, but they are what the Lord Jesus Himself willingly accepted from the day of His entrance into the world. Wealth ruins far more souls than poverty. When the love of money begins to creep over us let us think of the manger at Bethlehem, and of Him who was laid in it. Such thoughts may deliver us from much harm.

PRAYER

Royal King, Son of God, Saviour of the World, you became as poor as the very poorest, you became lowly as the very lowliest. I confess that I am easily tempted by the lure of money and possessions and am often envious of others. Remind me today of where my real treasure lies—that it lies in your love that is beyond understanding. It is unspeakable and unsearchable. From the hour of your birth to the hour of your death, you were poor for my sake. With my heart and soul, I give you thanks and praise. Amen.

DECEMBER 23

NO WORLDLY POMP
OR SHOW

READ LUKE 2:8–14

Now there were in the same country shepherds living out in the fields, keeping watch over their flock by night. And behold, an angel of the Lord stood before them, and ... said to them, "Do not be afraid, for behold, I bring you good tidings of great joy which will be to all people. For there is born to you this day in the city of David a Saviour, who is Christ the Lord." (2:8–11)

We read in these verses how the birth of the Lord Jesus was first announced to the world. The birth of a king's son is generally made an occasion of public celebration and rejoicing. The announcement of the birth of the Prince of Peace was made privately at midnight and without anything of worldly pomp and show.

Let us mark to whom the tidings first came that Christ was born. They were shepherds living out in the fields near Bethlehem, keeping watch over their flock by night. To shepherds—not to priests and rulers, not to Scribes and Pharisees—an angel appeared proclaiming, "there is born to you this day in the city of David a Saviour, who is Christ the Lord."

Let us also mark the language used by the angel in announcing Christ's birth to the shepherds. He said, "I bring you good tidings of great joy, which will be to all people."

We need not wonder at these words. The spiritual darkness which had covered the earth for four thousand years was about to be rolled away. The way to pardon and peace with God was about to be thrown open to all mankind. The head of Satan was about to be bruised. Liberty was about to be proclaimed to the captives and recovering of sight to the blind. The mighty truth was about to be proclaimed that God could be just and yet, for Christ's sake, justify the ungodly. Salvation was no longer to be seen through types and figures but openly and face to face.[3] The knowledge of God was no longer to be confined to the Jews, but to be offered to the whole Gentile world. The days of ignorance of the true God were numbered. The first stone of God's kingdom was about to be set up. If this was not "good tidings," there never were tidings that deserved the name.

PRAYER

Gracious Heavenly Father, you did not announce your Son's birth to princes and rulers, nor to religious and important people. You sent your angel to working men out in the fields. To them you proclaimed the way of pardon and peace, and your promise of liberty and salvation. Good tidings of great joy! Thank you that you reveal yourself to the last, the least and the lost. You are mindful of all, whether rich or poor, of high or low standing in our world. Forgive me when I prefer to give my attention to those of "higher standing" and when I am seduced by worldly pomp and show. I rejoice in you and your kindness today. Amen.

---

3   For definition of 'types', see the reading for December 19.

THE ANGELS' SONG

READ LUKE 2:8–14

And suddenly there was with the angel a multitude of the heavenly host praising God and saying: "Glory to God in the highest, and on earth peace, goodwill toward men!" (2:13–14)

Let us mark the hymn of praise which the heavenly host sung in the hearing of the shepherds. They said, "Glory to God in the highest, and on earth peace, goodwill toward men!"

"Glory to God in the highest!" the song begins. Now is come the highest degree of glory to God, by the appearing of His Son Jesus Christ in the world. He, by His life and death on the cross, will glorify God's attributes (justice, holiness, mercy and wisdom) as they never were glorified before. Creation glorified God, but not so much as redemption.

"Peace on earth!" the song goes on. Now is come to earth the peace of God which passes all understanding, the perfect peace between a holy God and sinful men and women which Christ was to purchase with His own blood, the peace which is offered freely to all, the peace which, once admitted into the heart, makes men and women live at peace one with another and will one day overspread the whole world.

"Goodwill towards men!" the song concludes. Now is come the time when God's kindness and good will towards guilty men and women is to be fully made known. His power was seen in creation, His justice was seen in the flood, but His mercy remained to be fully revealed by the appearing and atonement of Jesus Christ.

Such was the meaning of the angels' song. Happy are they that can enter into that meaning and, with their hearts, assent to its contents. The man who hopes to live in heaven should have some practical acquaintance with the language of its inhabitants.

PRAYER

Heavenly Father, I join in with the hymn of praise of the heavenly host. I worship you on this Christmas Eve, choosing you as my first priority today, above the glitter and busyness of the season.

Glory to God in the highest heaven! Your Son's birth, life and death reveal your justice, your holiness, your mercy and your wisdom. I praise you!

Peace on earth! Your Son has bought a peace which passes all understanding, peace between a holy God and sinful men and women. May that peace rest in my heart today as I keep my eyes fixed on you.

Goodwill towards men! Your kindness and mercy to us in Christ is beyond words. I praise you and bless you. Amen.

THE SHEPHERDS AND THE WISE MEN

READ LUKE 2:15–20 AND MATTHEW 2:1–12

And [the shepherds] came with haste and found Mary and Joseph, and the Babe lying in a manger. Now when they had seen Him, they made widely known the saying which was told them concerning this Child. (Luke 2:16–17)

Let us mark the prompt obedience to the heavenly vision displayed by the shepherds. We see in them no doubts, questionings or hesitation. Strange and improbable as the tidings might seem, they at once act upon them. They went to Bethlehem in haste and found everything exactly as they had been told. Their simple faith received a rich reward. They had the mighty privilege of being the very first people, after Mary and Joseph, who saw with believing eyes the new-born Messiah. They soon returned, glorifying and praising God for what they had seen.

May our spirit be like theirs! May we ever believe implicitly, act promptly and wait for nothing when the path of duty is clear! In so doing, we will have a reward like that of the shepherds. The journey that is begun in faith will generally end in praise.

> *Wise men from the East came to Jerusalem, saying, "Where is He who has been born King of the Jews? For we have seen His star in the East and have come to worship Him." (Matthew 2:1–2)*

Last, but not least, the behaviour of the wise men is a striking example of faith. They believed in Christ when they had never seen Him, but that was not all. They believed in Him when the Scribes and Pharisees were unbelieving, but again that was not all. They believed in Him when they saw Him a little infant on Mary's knee, and worshipped Him as a king. This was the crowning point of their faith. They saw no miracles to convince them, they heard no teaching to persuade them. They saw no signs of divinity and greatness to overawe them. They saw nothing but a new-born infant, helpless and weak, and needing a mother's care like any one of us. And yet when they saw that infant, they believed that they saw the divine Saviour of the world: they "fell down and worshipped Him."

This is the kind of faith, let us remember, that God delights to honour. We see the proof of that in our own day. Wherever the Bible is read, the actions of these wise men is known and told as a memorial of them. Let us walk in the steps of their faith. Let us not be ashamed to believe in Jesus and confess Him, though all around us remain careless and unbelieving. Have we not a thousand-fold more evidence than the wise men had, to make us believe that Jesus is the Christ? Beyond doubt we have.

PRAYER

Gracious Lord Jesus Christ, you came that first Christmas in weakness—unnoticed, unhonoured and scarcely known. You will come again in royal dignity, with the armies of heaven around you, to be known, recognised and worshipped by all the people of the earth.

Stir my heart to worship you in gratitude and awe today. Help me to make your good news widely known, as the shepherds did. May my faith be wholehearted and bold like that of the wise men. Please help me to love and serve you all the days of my life—or until you come again. Amen.